Grea

of the Bible

∾

Mary, the Mother of Jesus;
Women Who Served Jesus;
Women Whom Jesus Helped;
Women Who Helped the Apostles

CONCORDIA PUBLISHING HOUSE · SAINT LOUIS

Copyright © 2008 Concordia Publishing House
3558 S. Jefferson Avenue, St. Louis, MO 63118-3968
1-800-325-3040 · cph.org

Scripture quotations are from the ESV® Bible (The Holy Bible, English Standard Version®), copyright © 2001 by Crossway, a publishing ministry of Good News Publishers. Used by permission. All rights reserved.

Hymn texts with the abbreviation *LSB* are from the *Lutheran Service Book*, copyright © 2006 by Concordia Publishing House. All rights reserved.

This publication may be available in Braille, in large print, or on cassette tape for the visually impaired. Please allow 8 to 12 weeks for delivery. Write to Lutheran Braille Workers, P.O. Box 5000, Yucaipa, CA 92399; call toll-free 1-800-925-6092; or visit the website: www.LBWinc.org.

Manufactured in the United States of America

5   6   7   8   9   10   11   12   13   14   32 31 30 29 28 27 26 25 24 23 22

Contents

Hymnal Key

LSB = Lutheran Service Book
ELH = Evangelical Lutheran Hymnary
CW = Christian Worship
LW = Lutheran Worship
LBW = Lutheran Book of Worship
TLH = The Lutheran Hymnal

About This Series

Do you realize how often women are mentioned in the Bible? Do names like Eve, Sarah, Deborah, Ruth, Esther, Mary the mother of Jesus, Anna, Mary and Martha, Lydia, and Eunice and Lois sound familiar? They should. These are only a few of the great women mentioned in Holy Scripture.

The Bible not only gives us the names of these great women, but also describes their sorrows and joys, their defeats and victories, their intense private moments and important public duties. In contrast to the inaccurate myth that the Bible is an antiquated piece of antiwoman (misogynistic) literature, the Bible portrays women as God's creatures, different yet fully equal with men, fallen in sin yet redeemed by the precious blood of the Lamb.

In addition to sharing the thoughts, dreams, words, and deeds of women in the past, the Bible also provides helpful instruction for women of today. It encourages thrift and industry (Proverbs 31:10–31), teaches about healthy relationships between husbands and wives (Ephesians 5:22–33; Colossians 3:18–19), provides instruction in the relationship between older and younger women (Titus 2:3–5), celebrates the equality in diversity among believers (Galatians 3:28–29), and extols the important and varied roles women play in the partnership of the Gospel (Philippians 4:3).

Women can learn much about themselves in the Bible. But it would be a mistake to assume that what the Bible teaches about women is of no importance to men. In His Word, God unfolds for the believer both true womanhood and true manhood as He designed them, so that both sexes are affirmed in their equality and in their differences as God created them.

In this series, we cannot learn all there is to know about every great woman of the Bible. However, as we study God's Word, we can learn much about ourselves and our gracious Lord and how He worked in the lives of the great women of the Bible.

Suggestions for Small-Group Participants

1. Before you begin, spend some time in prayer, asking God to strengthen your faith through a study of His Word. The Scriptures were written so that we might believe in Jesus Christ and have life in His name (John 20:31).

2. Even if you are not the small-group leader, take some time prior to the meeting to look over the session, read the Bible verses, and answer the questions.

3. As a courtesy to others, be sure to arrive at each session on time.

4. Be an active participant. The leader is there to facilitate group discussion, not give a lecture.

5. Avoid dominating the conversation by answering each question or by giving unnecessarily long answers. Avoid the temptation to not share at all.

6. Treat anything shared in your group as confidential until you have asked for and received permission to share it outside of the group. Treat information about others outside of your group as confidential until you have asked for and received permission to share it inside of your group.

7. Realize that some participants may be new to the group or new to the Christian faith. Help them to feel welcomed and comfortable.

8. Affirm other participants when you can. If another participant offers what you perceive to be a "wrong" answer, ask the Holy Spirit to guide that person to seek the correct answer from God's Word.

9. Keep in mind that the questions are discussion starters. Don't be afraid to ask additional questions that relate to the session. Avoid getting the group off track.

10. If you feel comfortable doing so, now and then volunteer to pray either at the beginning or at the conclusion of the session.

Suggestions for Small-Group Leaders

1. Before you begin, spend some time in prayer, asking God to strengthen your faith through a study of His Word. The Scriptures were written so that we might believe in Jesus Christ and have life in His name (John 20:31). Also, pray for participants by name.

2. See the Leader Guide at the back of this study. It will help guide you in discovering the truths of God's Word. It is, however, neither exhaustive nor designed to be read aloud during your session.

3. Prior to your meeting, familiarize yourself with each session by reviewing the session material, reading the Bible passages, and answering the questions in the spaces provided. Your familiarity with the session will give you confidence as you lead the group.

4. As a courtesy to participants, begin and end each session on time.

5. Have a Bible dictionary or similar resource handy in order to look up difficult or unfamiliar names, words, and places. Ask participants to help you in this task. Be sure that each participant has a Bible and a study guide.

6. Ask for volunteers to read introductory paragraphs and Bible passages. A simple "thank you" will encourage them to volunteer again.

7. See your role as a conversation facilitator rather than as a lecturer. Don't be afraid to give participants time to answer questions. By name, thank each participant who answers; then ask for other participants. For example, you may say, "Thank you, Maggie. Would anyone else like to share?"

8. Now and then, summarize aloud what the group has learned by studying God's Word.

9. Keep in mind that the questions provided are discussion starters. Allow participants to ask questions that relate to the session. However, keep discussions on track.

10. Everyone is a learner! If you don't know the answer to a question, simply tell participants that you need time to look at more Scripture passages, or to ask your pastor, director of Christian education, or other lay leader. You can provide an answer at the next session.

11. Begin each session with prayer. Conclude each session with prayer. Ask for volunteers for these duties, and thank them for their participation. A suggested hymn is included at the end of each session. You may choose another hymn or song if you wish.

12. Encourage participants to read or reread the Scripture passages provided at the end of the session and, as they have time, to commit passages to memory.

❧

Mary, the Mother of Jesus

Our series now presents the great women of the New Testament. The first woman we meet in the Gospels is Elizabeth, the mother of John the Baptist. What little is said about her is partly interwoven with the story of her more famous relative, the Virgin Mary.

Of all the women mentioned in the Bible and in history, the best known and most highly honored is the mother of our Lord. Even the angel of God addressed her as "favored one." That is because God honored her to become the human mother of His divine Son. Although she was a sinful human being, Mary was the only woman to give birth to a sinless and perfect Son, who was true God and true man and as such could be the only Savior of all sinners.

Mary, the Favored One

We first meet Mary in her hometown of Nazareth. She is a young virgin girl engaged to marry a carpenter by the name of Joseph. One day, Mary is visited by the angel Gabriel, who announces, "Greetings, O favored one, the Lord is with you!" (see Luke 1:26–33).

1. Describe Mary's reaction to this announcement. Do you think her response was normal, given the circumstances? When have you been "greatly troubled" upon hearing what was ultimately good news?

Joseph, Jesus' foster father, was a legal descendant of David (Matthew 1:1–17; Luke 1:27; 3:23–31). Mary likewise was a descendant of the house of David (Romans 1:3). Thus, legally and physically, Jesus was David's heir.

2. What had become of David's royal family at the time of Mary (Isaiah 11:1–10, 53; Romans 15:8–12)? Do you attach importance to your genealogy or ancestry? Why or why not?

Since she was still a virgin, Mary was perplexed over the announcement about her giving birth (she and Joseph had yet to consummate their marriage). Nevertheless, she gave her consent to God's Word spoken by His messenger (Luke 1:34–38).

3. How did Mary give evidence of a strong faith and her willing submission to God's will (v. 38)?

4. Describe Mary's visit with her relative Elizabeth (Luke 1:39–45). How might this visit have benefited them both? If you feel comfortable, share when you have been comforted by someone undergoing a similar experience.

Mary's great hymn, known as the Magnificat (mag-NIH-fih-kaht; Luke 1:46–55), is sung in Vespers and Evening Prayer (see *Lutheran Service Book*, pp. 231–32, 248–49).

5. What thoughts does Mary express in her hymn? How does she state her need of God's grace and mercy?

6. What are we told about Mary's marriage to Joseph (Matthew 1:24–25)?

Mary, the Mother of Our Savior

Jesus was circumcised and named on the eighth day. On the fortieth day, Mary and Joseph brought Jesus to the temple so that Mary could perform her duties under the Law (Luke 2:21–24; see also Luke 1:31).

7. Which of God's Old Testament laws did Mary observe after the birth of her Son (see Leviticus 12)? How has Christ set us free from ceremonial laws such as these (see Galatians 4:4–5)?

While they were in the temple, two devout believers, Simeon and Anna, approached the holy family (Luke 2:25–38). We sing Simeon's song (vv. 29–32) in the Divine Service (see *Lutheran Service Book*, pp. 182, 199–200).

8. How did Simeon's praise and blessing prepare Mary for a tragic experience in her life (v. 35; see also John 19:25)? If you feel comfortable, describe a bittersweet experience in your life.

9. How might Mary have felt during the visit of the Magi (Matthew 2:1–12)?

We get a glimpse into the family life of Mary, Joseph, and Jesus during an annual visit to Jerusalem for the Passover (Luke 2:41–52). Faithfulness to God's Word, reliance on His promises, obedience to one's parents, and care and concern for each other are evident.

10. In what respects does the home life of the holy family serve as a model for all Christian homes? What can Christian parents do to ensure that their homes are filled with faith and love?

Mary, the Loyal Disciple

As children grow and mature, their relationships with their parents change. We see this in the account of a wedding banquet at Cana, in which our Lord performs His first miracle—at the request of His mother (John 2:1–12).

11. Why do you suppose Jesus called His beloved mother "woman"? Why did Mary tell the servants to do whatever Jesus told them (v. 5)? What did she learn about her Son at that wedding?

Jesus' loving mother expressed concern about His well-being. On one occasion, she and other family members demonstrated that concern while He was conducting His ministry (Mark 3:3–34).

12. How is the relationship that all believers, including Mary, have with Jesus through faith more important than His earthly familial relationships (see also Luke 11:27–28)?

13. Where did Mary make her home during our Lord's public ministry (John 2:12)? How might she have assisted Him?

Undoubtedly, Mary's greatest sorrow occurred during the trial, torture, crucifixion, and death of her Son (John 19:23–27; review Luke 2:35). Despite His immense suffering and pain, Jesus provided for His mother's continued care before His death on the cross (John 19:26–27).

14. Christ bore His cross and thus won for us the forgiveness of sins, life, and salvation. How can we, like Mary and Paul, bear our crosses relying on God's strength (see 2 Corinthians 12:8–10)?

Undoubtedly, Mary saw Jesus following His bodily resurrection from the dead (see 1 Corinthians 15:6). As with His other disciples, Mary's Good Friday grief turned into Easter joy.

15. The last picture of Mary that the New Testament gives us is found in Acts 1:14. How does Mary's life provide an example for all believers?

Other Women of That Period

16. In what ways were Elizabeth's life and experience similar to her cousin Mary's (see Luke 1:5–25, 39–45, 57–66; 3:1–6; Mark 6:14–29)?

17. How is Anna described in Luke 2:36–38 (see also 1 Timothy 5:5)? Is one's age a barrier to telling others about Christ?

Closing Worship

Close by reading/singing together the words of the Magnificat (*LSB*, pp. 231–32, 248–49).

Refrain:
My soul magnifies the Lord,
  and my spirit rejoices in God, my Savior.
My soul magnifies the Lord,
  and my spirit rejoices in God, my Savior.

For He has regarded
  the lowliness of His handmaiden.
For behold, from this day
  all generations will call me blessèd.

For the Mighty One has done great things to me,
  and holy is His name;
and His mercy is on those who fear Him
  from generation to generation.
Refrain

He has shown strength with His arm;
  He has scattered the proud in the imagination of their
    hearts.
He has cast down the mighty from their thrones
  and has exalted the lowly.

He has filled the hungry with good things,
  and the rich He has sent empty away.
He has helped His servant Israel in remembrance of His mercy
  as He spoke to our fathers, to Abraham and to his seed for-
    ever.

Glory be to the Father and to the Son
  and to the Holy Spirit;
as it was in the beginning,
  is now, and will be forever. Amen.
Refrain

For Daily Bible Reading

Monday: Luke 1
Tuesday: Luke 2
Wednesday: Matthew 2
Thursday: John 2:1–12
Friday: Matthew 12:38–50
Saturday: John 19:17–30
Sunday: Acts 1:1–14
For memorization: Luke 1:35, 37, 46–50; 11:28;
John 19:26–27; Acts 1:14

✧ Women Who Served Jesus

Jesus selected twelve men to be His apostles (Matthew 10:1–4). But among the wider circle of His disciples were also a number of women. Some of these had been helped and honored by the Lord, and they showed their gratitude by serving Him and His disciples. Some occasionally accompanied Him on His journeys. Others entertained Him in their homes or performed some special service for Him.

When all but one of our Lord's apostles deserted Him, it was women who remained near Him at the cross and watched His burial (John 19:25–27, 35; see also Mark 15:47). The first disciples to see the risen Savior and to testify about His resurrection were faithful women. We will now see how much Jesus meant to His women disciples and how closely they remained attached to Him.

Peter's Mother-in-Law

All we know about Peter's mother-in-law is found in a few brief Bible verses (Mark 1:30–31; see also Matthew 8:14–15; Luke 4:38–39). Following the example of Peter and others, pastors have a right to be married if they wish (1 Corinthians 9:5).

18. How did Peter apparently regard his mother-in-law (Mark 1:30)? How should Christian spouses treat their parents-in-law?

19. How did Peter's mother-in-law show her gratitude toward Jesus after He healed her? What are some ways that we can show our thankfulness to the Lord after He has restored our health?

Mary and Martha

Along with their brother, Lazarus, Mary and Martha were among Jesus' closest friends (John 11:5, 35–36). These siblings lived together in the village of Bethany, and in their home Jesus was welcomed and received their hospitality (Luke 10:38–42).

20. How did Mary and Martha show their love and regard for Jesus (vv. 39–40)? How did He teach Martha that receiving God's Word by faith takes precedence over doing good deeds (vv. 41–42)? When are we like Martha? like Mary?

John 11:1–44 records Jesus' raising of Lazarus from the dead. In this passage, we hear a clear confession of faith in Jesus as God's Messiah and in the resurrection of the dead.

21. How did Martha demonstrate her strong faith in Jesus (vv. 20–27)? What value does Lazarus's resurrection have for us today (vv. 33–44)?

22. We find Jesus at Mary and Martha's home one last time (John 12:1–3). How did they serve the Lord on this occasion (vv. 2–3)? How will God reward the good works we do in Christ's name (see Matthew 25:31–40; Hebrews 6:10; see also Luke 17:9–11)?

Mary Magdalene

Another faithful disciple of the Lord was Mary of Magdala. Magdala was a small fishing village on the Sea of Galilee. Despite a longstanding myth about her, Mary was not the immoral woman described in Luke 7:37–50.

23. How did Mary Magdalene become a disciple of Jesus (Luke 8:2–3)? How did she show her gratitude toward Him for her deliverance?

Mary Magdalene was among the faithful women who witnessed the crucifixion and burial of Jesus (Mark 15:40, 47).

24. What great honor did our Lord bestow upon Mary (Mark 16:1–10; John 20:1–18)? Discuss how experiencing our risen Lord in His Word and Sacraments likewise inspires and enables us to proclaim His resurrection to others.

25. How may Mary Magdalene have been a feminine counterpart to Peter in the circle of the disciples? What similar traits did she possess?

Other Women Disciples

26. Another faithful follower of Jesus was Salome, the wife of Zebedee and the mother of James and John. What does the Bible tell us about her (Matthew 20:20–28; 27:55–56; Mark 16:1)?

27. *Mary* was a common name in the New Testament era. Mary, the wife of Clopas, is sometimes referred to as "the other Mary." How was she related to Jesus (John 19:25)?

28. Joanna, the wife of Chuza, Herod's household manager, and Susanna financially supported the Lord's ministry (Luke 8:3; see also 24:10). How might your small group provide assistance to mission work, both at home and abroad?

29. Jesus lovingly and truthfully engaged a Samaritan woman at a well (John 4:3–42). How did she become an energetic missionary for Christ? Discuss how such an attitude is possible even today.

30. What interest did Pilate's wife show in Jesus (Matthew 27:19)? How may she have influenced her husband (v. 24)? Why should we seek to do good in all circumstances?

Closing Worship

Close by reading/singing together the words of "The Day of Resurrection" (*LSB* 478; *LW* 133; *TLH* 205; *CW* 166; *LBW* 141).

The day of resurrection!
    Earth, tell it out abroad,
The passover of gladness,
    The passover of God.
From death to life eternal,
    From sin's dominion free,
Our Christ has brought us over
    With hymns of victory.

Let hearts be purged of evil
    That we may see aright
The Lord in rays eternal
    Of resurrection light
And, list'ning to His accents,
    May hear, so calm and plain,

His own "All hail!" and, hearing,
  May raise the victor strain.

Now let the heav'ns be joyful,
  Let earth its song begin,
Let all the world keep triumph
  And all that is therein.
Let all things, seen and unseen,
  Their notes of gladness blend;
For Christ the Lord has risen,
  Our joy that has no end!

All praise to God the Father,
  All praise to God the Son,
All praise to God the Spirit,
  Eternal Three in One!
Let all the ransomed number
  Fall down before the throne
And honor, pow'r, and glory
  Ascribe to God alone!

John of Damascus, c. 696–c. 754; tr. John Mason Neale, 1818–66, alt.
Public domain

For Daily Bible Reading

Monday: Mark 1:29–39
Tuesday: Luke 10:38–42
Wednesday: John 11:1–45
Thursday: John 12:1–8
Friday: Mark 15:37–16:11
Saturday: John 20:1–18
Sunday: John 4:3–42
For memorization: Luke 10:41–42; John 4:42; 11:25–27;
20:16–17

∽ঌ

Women Whom Jesus Helped

The Gospels show that Jesus is the greatest friend and benefactor of women. They frequently record how Jesus helped women out of great physical or spiritual trouble.

Many of them experienced His healing power in that He cured either them or some dear relative from an otherwise incurable bodily affliction. Others He delivered out of a life of sin and shame and enabled to enjoy the peace and happiness that only the assurance of God's forgiveness can give a sinner.

When we read the four Gospels, we should note that Jesus gave special attention to the needs of women and raised them to a position of high honor.

The Syrophoenician Woman

Wanting to avoid opposition in Galilee and taking the opportunity to teach His disciples in private, Jesus traveled with them to Tyre. Tyre was a Gentile city about 30 miles from Capernaum.

31. A Syrophoenician woman, a pagan, begged Jesus to heal her daughter of demonic possession (Mark 7:24–30). How did she address Jesus, according to Matthew 15:22? How do you address the Lord in prayer when under duress?

At first, Jesus appeared to ignore the woman's request. However, there was a purpose behind His actions: to teach that the Gospel was first to be given to the Jews (Matthew 15:24).

32. Having been called the equivalent of a "little puppy" (v. 27), what was the woman's response (Mark 7:28)? How did this give evidence of her strong faith?

33. Jesus graciously delivered the woman's daughter from demonic possession (Mark 7:29–30). Why may God delay answering our prayers?

Women Healed by Jesus' Touch

Returning to Capernaum, Jesus was surrounded by a crowd near the lake. Hiding herself in the crowd, a woman who had hemorrhaged for twelve years touched Jesus' clothing and was instantaneously healed (Mark 5:21–43).

34. In addition to her ailment, the woman was ceremonially unclean (see Leviticus 15:25–33). What was Jesus' response to her humble confession (v. 34)? How should the Church respond to the sick or those who need the Lord's forgiveness?

Intertwined with this story of the woman's healing is the story of the healing of Jairus's twelve-year-old daughter (see also Matthew 9:18–26 and Luke 8:41–56).

35. Jesus went to Jairus's home and was greeted by loud, wailing mourners. Contrast their attitudes in verses 40 and 42.

Women Whom Jesus Forgave

A Pharisee, Simon, invited Jesus to his home, perhaps to entrap him. Nevertheless, Jesus accepted the invitation. There, an immoral woman, possibly a prostitute, entered Simon's home and anointed Jesus' feet with her tears and sweet-smelling perfume (Luke 7:36–50).

36. Apply Jesus' parable (vv. 40–43) to Simon and the woman. Who gave greater evidence of repentance (vv. 44–48)? When do we Christians hear, like the woman heard from Jesus (vv. 48–50), that our sins are forgiven?

Jesus absolved a woman caught in adultery (John 8:2–11). On this occasion, the Pharisees sought to stone the woman and to entrap our Lord.

37. Why did Jesus not condemn her? What warning did He give to her (v. 11)? What can the Church do to call people who have fallen into sexual and other sins to repentance and restoration?

Other Women Whom Jesus Helped or Honored

38. How did Jesus help the grief-stricken widow of Nain (Luke 7:11–17)? What does Jesus do for us in days of sorrow and tribulation (Matthew 11:28–29)?

39. Discuss Jesus' healing of the woman in a synagogue (Luke 13:10–17). What was the reaction of His chief critic (v. 14)? How does a legalistic attitude affect other sisters and brothers in Christ?

40. How did Jesus respond when mothers brought their babies and infants to Him (Mark 10:13–16)? What does this teach parents about Baptism, prayer and Bible stories in the home, and attendance at corporate Christian worship?

41. Jesus observed the faithful widow, who gave her last two mites to the Lord (Mark 12:41–44; Luke 21:1–4). When do we truly practice Christian stewardship?

42. What does Jesus teach us about prayer in His parable about the persistent widow (Luke 18:1–8)?

Closing Worship

Close by reading/singing together the words of "Entrust Your Days and Burdens" (*LSB* 754; *LW* 427; *TLH* 520).

Entrust your days and burdens
    To God's most loving hand;
He cares for you while ruling
    The sky, the sea, the land.
For He who guides the tempests
    Along their thund'rous ways
Will find for you a pathway
    And guide you all your days.

Rely on God your Savior
    And find your life secure.
Make His work your foundation

That your work may endure.
No anxious thought, no worry,
    No self-tormenting care
Can win your Father's favor;
    His heart is moved by prayer.

Take heart, have hope, my spirit,
    And do not be dismayed;
God helps in ev'ry trial
    And makes you unafraid.
Await His time with patience
    Through darkest hours of night
Until the sun you hoped for
    Delights your eager sight.

Leave all to His direction;
    His wisdom rules for you
In ways to rouse your wonder
    At all His love can do.
Soon He, His promise keeping,
    With wonder-working pow'rs
Will banish from your spirit
    What gave you troubled hours.

O blessèd heir of heaven,
    You'll hear the song resound
Of endless jubilation
    When you with life are crowned.
In your right hand your maker
    Will place the victor's palm,
And you will thank Him gladly
    With heaven's joyful psalm.

Our hands and feet, Lord, strengthen;
    With joy our spirits bless
Until we see the ending
    Of all our life's distress.
And so throughout our lifetime
    Keep us within Your care

And at our end then bring us
To heav'n to praise You there.

For Daily Bible Reading

Monday: Matthew 15:21–28; Mark 7:24–30
Tuesday: Matthew 9:18–26; Mark 5:22–43
Wednesday: Luke 8:41–56
Thursday: Luke 7:36–50; John 8:1–11
Friday: Luke 7:11–17; 13:10–17
Saturday: Mark 10:13–16; 12:41–44
Sunday: Matthew 25:1–13
For memorization: Matthew 11:28; Luke 7:13, 50; 8:48;
15:10; 18:16; 19:10; John 14:13

❧
Women Who Helped
the Apostles

The first Christian congregations consisted of both women and men. The women in the Early Church not only worshiped God in the public services, but also supported the Church with their means. As active missionaries, they helped to spread the Gospel. Some gave up their possessions and homes, some even their lives, for the sake of Jesus.

In the Book of Acts and in the Epistles, we encounter the names of some Christian women who were of great help to the apostles in establishing and building Christian congregations and in making Christ known to all people.

Tabitha, a Friend of the Poor

The Gospel was brought to Samaria first by Philip (Acts 8:5–8, 26–40), and then by Peter (9:32–10:48). Tabitha ("Dorcas" in Greek) was a Samaritan disciple in Joppa (9:36), an ancient port city on the Mediterranean Sea.

43. Why was Tabitha honored and well-liked (Acts 9:36, 39)? How can you be a Tabitha in your community or serve with other women in a Dorcas society?

Tabitha's death was a heavy blow to the community. Immediately, the Church in Joppa asked Peter to leave Lydda and come to help them.

44. How was Tabitha brought back to life? Ultimately, what is the purpose of all miracles accomplished in Christ's name (Acts 9:42; see also Luke 24:46–47)?

Lydia, a Businesswoman

Paul received a vision telling him to preach the Gospel in Macedonia (Acts 16:9). Because there was no synagogue in Philippi, worshipers of the true God gathered at the Gangites River. There Paul met a wealthy businesswoman named Lydia (vv. 13–15).

45. Through Paul's preaching, God gave Lydia faith in Christ. How did she show her gratitude for becoming a Christian (v. 15b)? List ways Christian women have supported and continue to support Christian missionaries and pastors.

After Paul and Silas were beaten and jailed for preaching the Gospel and delivering a woman possessed by a demon, they were miraculously released from prison (Acts 16:16–39). Lydia opened her home to them and other believers (v. 40).

46. The congregation in Philippi, of which Lydia was a charter member, was very dear to Paul. How did it assist him in his ministry in a way unlike other congregations (Philippians 4:15)?

Priscilla, a Great Church Worker

When Paul arrived in Corinth, he stayed at the home of Priscilla and Aquila, fellow believers and, like Paul, Jewish tentmakers (Acts 18:1–4).

47. Priscilla and Aquila accompanied Paul to Ephesus (Acts 18:18–19). How important were they to Paul's ministry (see Romans 16:3; 2 Timothy 4:19)?

Priscilla and Aquila showed hospitality to Apollos, a young Jewish man who was very knowledgeable in the Scriptures. Apollos knew only about John's Baptism (Acts 18:24–26).

48. Could we say that the first Christian seminary was founded in Priscilla and Aquila's home? How did Apollos later serve the Church (1 Corinthians 3:5–6; 16:12)?

When Paul wrote his Epistle to the Romans, Priscilla and Aquila were living there. Due to either their work or their service to the Gospel, they often changed their place of residence (see Acts 18:2; 1 Corinthians 16:19; 2 Timothy 4:19).

49. Apart from Acts 18:2 and 1 Corinthians 16:19, why do you suppose that Priscilla's name is mentioned in Scripture before her husband's? How does Paul praise Priscilla and Aquila in Romans 16:3–5?

Other Women in Acts and the Epistles

50. Sapphira, along with her husband, Ananias, suffered the Lord's chastisement for lying (Acts 5:1–10). Why does the Lord record such incidents in Scripture (see 1 Corinthians 10:11)?

51. What two women are mentioned in Acts 12:12–17? What is remarkable about the daughters of Philip the evangelist (Acts 21:9)?

52. Timothy was of mixed religious heritage (Acts 16:1). What role did his mother and grandmother play in his spiritual development (2 Timothy 1:5)? Why is it important that female relatives teach the faith to children?

53. A Philippian girl's demonic affliction was cruelly exploited for financial gain (Acts 16:16–18). What did it cost Paul to set her free (see vv. 19–24)?

54. Paul's sister is mentioned once in Scripture (Acts 23:16). What do we learn about the wives of the apostles (1 Corinthians 9:5; 7:8)?

55. What position did Phoebe hold in the Church (Romans 16:1–2)? List the other women greeted by Paul in Romans 16:3, 6, 12, 13, and 15.

56. What attitude should Christian women show toward one another (1 Corinthians 13:4–7; Ephesians 2:19–21)? Give practical ways this can be done in today's congregation.

Closing Worship

Close by reading/singing together the words of "Take My Life and Let It Be" (*LSB* 783; *LW* 404; *TLH* 400; *CW* 469; *LBW* 406; *ELH* 444).

Take my life and let it be
Consecrated, Lord, to Thee;
Take my moments and my days,
Let them flow in ceaseless praise.

Take my hands and let them move
At the impulse of Thy love;
Take my feet and let them be
Swift and beautiful for Thee.

Take my voice and let me sing
Always, only for my King;
Take my lips and let them be
Filled with messages from Thee.

Take my silver and my gold,
Not a mite would I withhold;
Take my intellect and use

Ev'ry pow'r as Thou shalt choose.

Take my will and make it Thine,
It shall be no longer mine;
Take my heart, it is Thine own,
It shall be Thy royal throne.

Take my love, my Lord, I pour
At Thy feet its treasure store;
Take myself, and I will be
Ever, only, all for Thee.

Frances R. Havergal, 1836–79
Public domain

For Daily Bible Reading

Monday: Acts 5:1–10; 9:36–43
Tuesday: Acts 12:1–17
Wednesday: Acts 16:1–40
Thursday: Acts 18:1–28
Friday: Romans 16
Saturday: Philippians 4
Sunday: 1 Corinthians 11:1–16; 2 John
For memorization: 1 Timothy 5:14; Proverbs 31:10, 25–28, 30

Leader Guide

Each one-hour session is divided into three to six subsections. Participants will first look at the life of the historical figure in the biblical text. Then they will be encouraged from what they read and discuss to make practical application to their own lives and situations.

Remember that this study is only a guide. Your role as group leader is to facilitate interaction between individual participants and the biblical text and among participants in your small group. By God's Spirit working through His Word, participants will learn and grow together.

Begin and end each session with prayer. Each session concludes with suggestions for weekly Bible readings, Bible memorization, and a hymn. You may choose a different hymn or song based on the needs of your group.

Mary, the Mother of Jesus

Women occupy a prominent place in the New Testament as well as in the Old Testament Scriptures. Our sessions will look at only the most important women mentioned in the Gospels and Acts. Less prominent women, such as Elizabeth, Anna, and many others, although great in their own way, will be discussed at the end of each session.

Although every Christian ought to be familiar with all that the Bible says about the Virgin Mary, the Mother of our Lord, it would be disappointing to omit her name from our present studies. What the Gospels tell us about Jesus is, of course, much more important than who Mary was and what she said and did. Nevertheless, there is no other woman in the Bible from whom Christian women can learn so much about the ideal of godly womanhood as from Mary.

Mary, the Favored One

1. The Bible is silent about Mary's youth, why she lived in Nazareth, and so on. She first appears as a virgin engaged to a carpenter by the name of Joseph. According to God's Word, Mary became the mother of the sinless Christ without the agency of a human father. The virgin birth is clearly set forth in Isaiah 7:14; Matthew 1:18–25; and Luke 1:26–37. If this were not true, we could have no Savior, for only a sinless, divine-human Christ could have atoned for our sins. Matthew 1:18–25 relays to us Joseph's thoughts about Mary's conception, misgivings that only a direct revelation from God could dispel.

The angel's words to Mary (Luke 1:26–37) should be carefully read and studied. Mary implicitly believed the Lord's words, but she realized what an embarrassing situation she would now have before the world. However, she trusted that God would preserve her honor and supply the solution to her problem. We can understand why Mary did not reveal the angel's message to Joseph but left it to God to inform him in due time. It must have been difficult keeping this secret.

2. The prophet Isaiah in the Old Testament and the apostle Paul in the New Testament indicate that David's royal family had dwindled down to very few people. Quoting Isaiah, Paul suggests that Jesus is the "root of Jesse" (Romans 15:12). No leaf, twig, branch, or trunk of David's family remained; Jesus' miraculous conception by the Holy Spirit through the Virgin Mary was as if He had sprung forth directly from David's father, Jesse.

Evidently, in Matthew 1 and Luke 3, we have the genealogy of Joseph (Christ's legal father). Since Christ was also to have been a direct descendant, by blood, of David, Mary had to be the connecting link (Romans 1:3). That both Mary and Joseph were of David's house makes Christ's fulfillment of this requirement unquestionable.

Allow participants to discuss with sensitivity whether knowing their lineage is important to them. Some participants may have been adopted or may not know their birth parents.

3. Ever since the first Gospel promise to Eve and Adam (Genesis 3:15), faithful women had been anticipating the birth of the Coming One, Abraham's Seed, the Messiah. Although the content of Gabriel's announcement was undoubtedly overwhelming, through God-given faith Mary believed this Word of God and accepted it. Mary's faith is evidenced by her willing and full-hearted response to the angel in Luke 1:38.

4. For Mary's own sake, it was wise that she left Nazareth for some time. Evidently, for her own consolation and strengthening, she decided to pay Elizabeth a visit. With this elderly woman (Luke 1:7), she could safely discuss her problems, and the two could relate their experiences with pregnancy. Fortunately, Elizabeth knew about Mary's situation through a special revelation from God (Luke 1:41–45).

Allow participants to discuss when they've been comforted by someone who has undergone a similar experience (pregnancy, an illness, relationship issues, etc.).

5. Mary's divinely inspired hymn of praise to God is one of the finest specimens of religious poetry. The Magnificat moves in the language of the Psalms and shows how well-versed Mary was in the Scriptures of the Old Testament. In it, note Mary's expressions of humility and her references to God's grace and mercy; her hymn is

one grand praise of God's mercy. In personal faith, she calls Him "my Savior" (v. 47).

6. What is said in Matthew 1:24–25 about the marriage of Joseph and Mary is highly significant. Joseph married her to shield her, but he denied himself the rights of a husband so that it could not be said that Jesus had a human father. Thus he showed Mary the highest honor and respect.

Mary, the Mother of Our Savior

7. Our Lord was circumcised and named on the eighth day according to Levitical law (Luke 2:21; Leviticus 12:3).

As a faithful member of God's people, Mary scrupulously observed all the laws of Moses that related to her personal life. She did not think of her own case as an exception to rules imposed upon ordinary mothers. When her time of purification was over, Mary offered a pair of doves as a sacrifice (Luke 2:21–24; Leviticus 12:4, 6–8). It was God's will that His Son should be put under the Law for our sakes (Galatians 4:4), so that we might be set free to live our lives in faith, enabled by His grace.

8. What Mary saw and heard in the temple served to strengthen her faith. But Simeon's prediction of her future great sorrow must have shaken this young mother (Luke 2:35). We wonder whether this word came to her mind again on that fateful Good Friday when she stood at her Son's cross.

Allow participants to share their bittersweet experiences and what eventually happened in those situations.

9. Although the Scriptures do not detail Mary's feelings at this time, the Magi (Matthew 2:1–12) must have amazed her. They arrived following Mary's return from the temple, at least forty days— if not several months—after the birth of Christ. Immediately after their departure, Mary and Joseph left for Egypt. Through the Magi, God supplied the holy family with money for their support in Egypt.

10. We would like to know much more about Jesus' boyhood and His early home life. However, all that God wants us to know is recorded in Luke 2:41–52. Here we see Mary acting like any other truly human mother and scolding her Son for having caused her anxiety. But here she got to know her Son as one altogether differ-

ent from all other children. In His first recorded words, she could catch the first flash of His divine nature (v. 49). His remarkable statement must have brought back to her mind many things about Him that she had forgotten (v. 51).

In this passage, we see that Mary and Joseph faithfully attended to the physical and spiritual needs of the boy Jesus. Allow participants to discuss what parents may do to ensure that their homes are truly faith- and love-filled.

Mary, the Loyal Disciple

11. Until He was thirty years old, Jesus lived and labored like any other man in His Nazareth home. Joseph had undoubtedly died during that time. We are not told about Jesus' departure from Mary's home when He went to visit John the Baptist and began His own ministry. Upon His return to Galilee, He found His mother attending a wedding at Cana. Possibly serving as a matron of honor, Mary brought the predicament of the scarcity of wine to His attention (John 2). Perhaps she thought that this was a good opportunity for Him to demonstrate His divine power. Verse 11 proves that this would be His first miracle.

Jesus' words to His beloved mother allowed her to understand that her relationship to Him had now changed. As His mother, she had no part to play in His public office. Yet, He did not harshly rebuff her, as the word "woman" may sound to us. From now on He treated Mary as one of His disciples. Mary seems to have understood, and she looked up to her Son in faith as her Lord, certain that He would help people in their need at the right time (v. 5).

12. Naturally, Mary and Jesus' other earthly relatives would have been concerned about Him, especially as He met with challenges in His earthly ministry. The incident in Mark 3, and Jesus' recorded response, shows that while Jesus' familial relationships were important to Him, of far greater importance was the eternal relationship God in love desired to restore through Jesus' life, death, and resurrection. Through faith in our Savior, we have an even deeper relationship with Jesus and other believers than we do with our parents, siblings, spouses, or closest friends.

13. Mary made her home with Jesus in Capernaum (John 2:12), the center of His public ministry. This home was evidently

home also to relatives of Mary. She probably did not accompany Jesus on His Galilean trips but may have gone with Him to Jerusalem; at least, she did this on His last journey, since we find her at the cross.

14. We note in John 19:25–27 the provision that the dying Savior on the cross made for His mother. He appointed John to take His place as the provider for her. Tradition holds that John cared for Mary in Ephesus until her death.

Both Mary and Paul are examples of God's powerful grace at work in the lives of believers, especially those whom God has called to suffer. Like it was for them, God's forgiving grace in His Word and Sacraments is sufficient to sustain us, whatever crosses we may bear.

15. Christ's mother is not mentioned in any of the Easter accounts, but we may assume that she was with the disciples and saw the resurrected Lord. This seems the more probable when we consider the reference to her in Acts 1:14, the last time her name is mentioned in the Bible. After praying with the disciples, she disappears from our view. Mary is never mentioned in the Epistles.

Mary provides an example to all believers, both women and men, of God's work in the life of a redeemed child of God. Faith in God's Son and obedient trust in His Word were her mainstays. May God grant us such grace and faith as He did Mary!

Other Women of That Period

16. Neither Elizabeth nor Mary had ever conceived or given birth to a child; their conceptions were by divine grace (although Mary's conception of Jesus was by the Holy Spirit and without the agency of a human father); the angel Gabriel announced the births of their sons (Mary received the announcement directly; Elizabeth through her husband, Zechariah); both their sons were called by God to specific ministries (Jesus as Savior of the world and John to prepare His way); and both their sons would die in the Lord's service.

17. Anna is described as a prophetess. She apparently lived at the temple and spent her time in continual worship and prayer. The topic of her witnesses to others was her Savior—the promised Messiah. At eighty-four, an advanced age even compared to today's

longer life spans, Anna was not deterred in speaking to others about Christ.

Women Who Served Jesus

Although numerous women are mentioned in the New Testament, in most cases they are presented with far less detail than is generally recorded in the Old Testament. Therefore, the remaining women of the New Testament have been divided into three groups: (1) women who served Jesus; (2) women whom Jesus helped in trouble; and (3) women who helped the apostles.

Peter's Mother-in-Law

18. Peter's mother-in-law deserves to receive special consideration because of her relationship to the apostle. Paul tells us that Peter's wife accompanied him on his missionary travels. Her name, however, is not mentioned, and nothing further is known about her. This we do know, however. During the time of Christ's ministry, Peter maintained a home in Capernaum. His wife's mother was a loved and respected member of that home. Her relatives and friends showed great concern about her when she became ill.

Here Peter provides us with a good example of loving care and concern for one's parents-in-law. Allow participants to cite specific examples of such care.

19. Jesus found Peter's mother-in-law ill with a fever. In answer to the prayers of her loved ones, He restored her immediately to perfect health. After suffering an extreme illness, many patients are weak for a long time after they show the initial signs of recovery. However, this woman was strong enough to help her daughter with the domestic duties of entertaining a large group of people. She was a woman who was eager to serve and to do what she could.

Many times Christians, having recovered from a specific illness, feel compelled to help others dealing with the same illness. Allow participants to explore other examples of serving.

Mary and Martha

20. Mary, Martha, and Lazarus were siblings. They lived in the same home in Bethany, a village on the east side of the Mount of Olives. The Bible doesn't discuss their marital status, but it is possible that either Mary or Martha was widowed or that financial hardship led to their living arrangement. Mary and Martha had different temperaments, but both believed that Jesus was the Messiah. They were happy to have Him in their home as their honored guest. Jesus loved to visit and rest in their home (see Luke 21:37).

On one occasion, Martha was so eager to show her high regard for Jesus that her good intentions received the Lord's rebuke (Luke 10:38–42). Jesus had come to teach them about His kingdom. Mary listened with attentive ears. Martha, on the other hand, thought it more important to get a good meal on the table. She was angry with Mary for not helping her and with Jesus because He did not seem to care. Martha meant well, but Jesus taught her (and all Christians) a very important lesson: hearing God's Word must not be neglected for the sake of earthly things, even those that on the surface appear pious or churchly. Martha took the lesson to heart, as the next chapter in her life proves.

21. John 11 records the familiar story of the resurrection of Lazarus, Mary and Martha's brother. When their brother became dangerously ill, the sisters quickly sent a message to Jesus, implying that they wished Him to come and make Lazarus well. But Jesus permitted Lazarus to die. He wanted to strengthen their faith and to perform a great miracle on their behalf. When they heard that Jesus was approaching Bethany, first Martha and then Mary went out to meet Him. Jesus spoke some of the most comforting words to Martha that ever came from His lips (vv. 25–26). Martha believed Him and gave a noble confession of her strong faith (v. 27). Although at the grave her faith began to waver (v. 39), Jesus gave her faith the support it needed (v. 40). In the resurrection of their brother, Mary and Martha had visible proof that Jesus is Lord over life and death.

Verses 33–34 continue today to strengthen our faith in our Savior who is God and Lord even over death and the grave. Through His cross and empty tomb, He has destroyed these our enemies forever.

22. Shortly before His death, Jesus was again entertained in Bethany (John 12). On this occasion, Martha once more served the bodily needs of Jesus, but this time in the right spirit. Mary again showed her interest in spiritual things by anointing Jesus in advance for His death and burial (vv. 3–8; Mark 14:3–9).

In His Word, God promises rewards for the good works that we do through faith in His Son. Allow participants to examine passages such as Matthew 25:31–40 and Hebrews 6:10 (see also Luke 17:9–11).

Mary Magdalene

23. Mary from Magdala became Jesus' disciple after He had released her from "seven demons" (Luke 8:2). In those days many people were tormented by evil spirits, for which the victims were not always to blame (see John 9:1–3).

In response, Mary Magdalene became one of the most devoted disciples of Jesus. She seems to have been a woman of means and, like others, to have used her money for the support of Jesus and His disciples (Luke 8:3).

24. Mary Magdalene occupies a prominent and honored position in the narratives of Christ's crucifixion and resurrection. She was one of the women who stood near the cross and also witnessed the burial of Jesus (Matthew 27:56, 61; Mark 15:40, 47; John 19:25). She helped the other women prepare spices to anoint the body of Jesus (Mark 16:1). The last to leave the grave of her Lord, she was also among the first to be at the empty tomb on Easter morning and the first to see the risen Savior (Mark 16:9; John 20:1–18).

Mary Magdalene has the honor of having been the first disciple to whom the risen Jesus revealed Himself (John 20:16). She was also the first messenger and missionary of the risen Lord to His disciples (Mark 16:10; John 20:17–18). Her great love for her Savior had kept her close to the cross and the sepulcher.

Like Mary, we too have been delivered from sin, the power of the devil, and death. Through Christ's death and resurrection, we have God's full pardon and the complete forgiveness of our sins. Through the Gospel and the Sacraments, God applies Christ's merits to us, which are received through the gift of faith. Having experienced our crucified and resurrected Lord, to whose death and resurrection we were united in our Baptism (Romans 6), we are inspired and enabled to tell others about Him and what He has done for us.

25. It has been said that in her zeal and fervor Mary Magdalene was much like Peter and that she held a position of leadership among the women disciples like that of Peter among the men. Her passionate fervor directed her to dedicate her life to Jesus.

Other Women Disciples

26. Comparing Bible passages, we can conclude that the name of Zebedee's wife was Salome. The apostles James and John were her two illustrious sons. She was ambitious, energetic, and quick to act. Undoubtedly, her sons put her up to asking Jesus for the highest places of honor in His kingdom (Matthew 20:20–28). However, when Jesus said, "You do not know what you are asking" (v. 22), He was speaking to them, not to her.

27. We meet six Marys in the New Testament. The "other Mary" of the Gospels, to distinguish her from the Virgin Mary, was the wife of Clopas (or Cleophas). Her sons were the apostle James (the Less) and Joses. She followed Jesus and gave her means for His needs. She may have been Jesus' aunt, the sister of His mother, Mary, or her sister-in-law (see John 19:25).

28. Joanna was the wife of Chuza, a steward of Herod the tetrarch (see Acts 13:1). All that we know about her and Susanna is that they served Jesus (Luke 8:3).

Allow participants to discuss how their small group can support both local and foreign missions.

29. The story of the woman of Samaria (John 4) beautifully displays the Lord's love for sinners, both in how He addresses their sins through the Law and in how He forgives their sins through the Gospel.

If there is time, allow participants to refamiliarize themselves with this story and apply what they learn to energetic mission work today.

30. While we have only a brief glimpse of Pilate's wife (Matthew 27:19), it is possible that her wifely warnings influenced him in his dealings with Jesus (see v. 24).

42

Allow participants to discuss how concern for justice and mercy can and should motivate us to do good for all people.

Women Whom Jesus Helped

In the Gospels, we read about many great women who helped Jesus in some way. Participants may be acquainted with some of them already through their previous study of God's Word. All of these stories show that Jesus wanted to be the Savior of all people and help everyone out of their physical and spiritual troubles regardless of sex or race. It is noteworthy that women were often the beneficiaries of His merciful acts and that He was particularly pleased with the faith and love they manifested toward Him. No higher honor can come to women than that which has been bestowed upon them by the Gospel (see Galatians 3:28–29).

The Syrophoenician Woman

31. The Syrophoenician woman (Matthew 15:21–28 and Mark 7:24–30) lived in Phoenicia, near the cities of Tyre and Sidon. Mark calls her a Greek (Gentile in the ESV), and Matthew called her a Canaanite; people of mixed races lived in Phoenicia. The strange thing about this pagan woman is that she had heard of Jesus and believed that He was the divine Savior for whom the Hebrews were waiting. Read again how she addressed Jesus in faith: "Have mercy on me, O Lord, Son of David" (v. 22).

Allow participants to discuss how they address the Lord in prayer (that is, what divine names or titles they use) during times of duress. For some, it may be as simple as this woman's, "O Lord."

32. The way Jesus treated this woman has puzzled many Christians. As far as we know, He had never otherwise ignored or refused to help anyone. In effect, Jesus was stating that He had come first for the Jews, God's "children" (v. 27), not a "little dog" like this Gentile woman. But instead of taking His remarks as an insult, the woman humbly admitted that she had no claim to His mercy. Nevertheless, she was sure that He could not deny her the crumbs of God's grace that He would have to spare. Jesus had purposely used a word that refers to little dogs that were kept as household pets, not stray dogs. The woman had faith and was keen

enough to note the difference and make use of this to catch Jesus in an argument of perfect logic (v. 28).

33. The woman, of course, acted just as Jesus wanted her to act. By their discourse, Jesus had exposed her strong faith for the benefit of His disciples.

God may delay answering our prayers for the purpose of strengthening our faith or the faith of others. Allow participants to discuss how they were strengthened by God's promises in His Word when an answer to their prayers did not seem imminent.

Women Healed by Jesus' Touch

34. Here we have a double story told by Matthew, Mark, and Luke. The woman had hemorrhaged for twelve years and was unable to find relief. This affliction made her Levitically unclean and caused her to avoid people. Participants will be able to understand her feelings and her reasons for shunning publicity.

Jesus' loving response to the woman (v. 34) is a beautiful illustration of God's rich mercy in Christ. The unclean person is made clean, the sick one is made well, the shunned sister is restored, and the sinner is forgiven.

Allow participants to discuss how the Church's response can and should mirror Jesus' response to this poor, sick woman when it comes to providing health care to the sick and the forgiveness of sins through the Gospel to the sinner.

35. The story of Jesus raising Jairus's daughter need not be treated at length. Nothing need be said about the father's efforts to save his child. The mother's name is not given, but she, her husband, and Jesus' closest disciples (Peter, James, and John) were in the child's room when Jesus raised her from the dead (Mark 5:40). What must this scene have meant to the heartbroken mother! The young girl surely never forgot what Jesus had done in restoring her life.

When Jesus mentioned that the child was only asleep (v. 39), the mourners laughed (v. 40). However, after He raised the child by His all-powerful Word, their mood changed into one of amazement (v. 42).

Women Whom Jesus Forgave

36. Luke 7:36–50 tells the story of a woman. While she is called a "sinner," what she had done is not explicitly stated. Perhaps she was a prostitute; Simon the Pharisee seems to have known her reputation. Simon was not a believer; his purpose in inviting Jesus to a meal seems to have been to entrap Him. Verse 39 shows how he felt toward Jesus.

Jesus exposed both Simon's hypocrisy and the woman's faith in Him through a brief parable (vv. 40–42). The sinful woman knew that she was a sinner, and in humble repentance she sought God's forgiveness and grace in Christ. She had true love for Jesus, because she had learned how greatly He loves sinners and what it means to be saved by Him (v. 47). Simon did not love Jesus, because he did not feel that he was a sinner who needed Christ's love. Previously she revealed her sinful heart by her public immorality; now by her public worship of Jesus (v. 38) she gives evidence of God's cleansing and forgiving grace in Him.

Today, we Christians hear that our sins are forgiven from Christ who speaks to us and forgives us through His Gospel and Sacraments.

37. The story of the adulteress in John 8:2–11 is somewhat similar to the one above. Her case also gave Christ the opportunity to warn the Pharisees about their hypocrisy. Jesus must have found her sincerely penitent, or He would not have dismissed her as kindly as He did. Such a person would, of course, need to be warned not to fall into sinful ways again (John 8:11). In the presence of the forgiving Jesus, she became a changed woman.

Allow participants to discuss what the Church can do to call people out of sexually immoral lifestyles—and other sinful lifestyles—to the restorative forgiveness that only Christ can offer.

Other Women Whom Jesus Helped or Honored

38. The Lord comforted the grief-stricken widow of Nain (Luke 11:13), then with His powerful Word raised her only son from the dead (v. 14). Likewise, the Lord comforts us in the midst of our sufferings and sadness and promises us a "rest" (Matthew 11:29) that only He can give.

39. In Luke 13:10–17, we read about Jesus healing a physically challenged woman with both His Word and touch. We also hear from a critic (notably the "ruler of the synagogue," v. 14), who complains that the healing violated the Sabbath. We Christians, too, can fall prey to such self-righteous and legalistic attitudes if we consider the needs of others less important than following rules or traditions not mandated by God's Word.

40. Jesus welcomed babies and infants into His presence (Mark 10:13–16; see also Matthew 19:13–15 and Luke 18:15–17).

Encourage participants to discuss the importance of parental initiative in the spiritual well-being of their children, beginning in infancy (see 2 Timothy 3:14–16). List also practical means by which this important work can be accomplished, beginning at home: reading Bible story books, mealtime and bedtime prayers, singing hymns and religious songs in the home, faithful Sunday School and church attendance, and such.

41. The incident of the "widow's mite" is recorded twice in Scripture. Jesus praises her because "she out of her poverty has put in everything she had, all she had to live on" (Mark 12:44).

Allow participants to discuss the meaning of practicing true Christian stewardship, based on Jesus' praise of this woman's strong faith, which yielded itself in faith-filled deeds (see also 2 Corinthians 9:7).

42. Just as He used the example of a poor woman to teach all Christians the meaning of true Christian stewardship, so too by the parable of the persistent widow (Luke 18:1–8), Jesus teaches all Christians, both women and men, the importance of persistent prayer (see also 1 Thessalonians 5:17–18).

Women Who Helped the Apostles

A considerable list of women may be drawn up from the Book of Acts and the Epistles, but of these only a few receive more than a passing mention. We are told repeatedly that in the first Christian congregations were many women believers (Acts 1:14; 6:1; 8:3; 12:12; 17:4, 12). That so many are mentioned by name indicates that these attained positions of influence and honor in the Early Church. Three women in particular should engage our attention because of the splendid service they rendered to the cause of the Gospel at a time when there were only a few Christians. These few had to endure the bitter opposition of a heathen world.

Tabitha, a Friend to the Poor

43. In Aramaic, *Tabitha* means "splendor, or beauty"; her Greek name, *Dorcas*, means "a doe, a graceful and beautiful creature." Tabitha was a Jewish person who had become a Christian when disciples carried the Gospel to Joppa (see Acts 8:4). She put her faith into practice by sewing for poor women (Acts 9:36, 39). She seems to have been the first woman who was driven by love for Christ to be active in such works of charity.

Allow participants to discuss how they as individuals or as a group can serve the needs in their community. *Dorcas* is a familiar name in many congregations for a group or society of women dedicated to such a purpose.

44. There was great sorrow among the poor in Joppa when Tabitha suddenly died. The disciples called for Peter (who was in nearby Lydda), and when he arrived, they showed him what Tabitha had done for them. Evidently, Tabitha had also shared her faith in Jesus and thus had been a benefactress not only of their bodies but also of their souls. Peter knelt and prayed before speaking to her (Acts 9:40) and helping her with his hand (v. 41). Through her, the attention of many was attracted to Christianity (v.

42). God used Peter to restore Tabitha to life not only for her sake but also to open new doors to the Gospel (participants may review Luke 24:46–47).

Lydia, a Businesswoman

45. Paul had seen in a vision a man calling him to bring the Gospel to Macedonia (Acts 16:9). When he came to Europe, his first convert was a woman named Lydia. She was a businesswoman who had formerly lived in Thyatira, a city in Asia Minor, which was famous for its dyes ("purple goods," v. 14). She had moved to Philippi, where she did a flourishing business selling the costly fabric. We do not know whether she was married or had become a widow. Her "household" must have included a number of servants, and she seems to have lived in comfortable circumstances.

Lydia was among a group of Jewish women to whom Paul first, after his arrival in Europe, preached the Gospel. He met these women outside the city of Philippi at the Gangas (or Gangites) River, where they seem to have met for worship. Lydia soon became a Christian and requested Baptism for herself and her household (which may have included children—if not her own, then those of her servants). She invited Paul and his companions to stay at her house, thus giving evidence of her sincere gratitude and strong faith (v. 15).

Here it would be helpful for participants to discuss, in detail if possible, the many and various ways women have worked (oftentimes without recognition) toward the support of Christian missionaries and pastors.

46. For a miracle that they had performed on an unfortunate girl, Paul and Silas were thrown into prison in Philippi (Acts 16). Here Paul was able to convert the jailer. After God had set His missionaries free again, they returned to the house of Lydia, which apparently had become the first meeting place of the congregation in Philippi (v. 40). Her home thus became one of the first of countless Christian homes in which congregations were founded and church services held until special houses of worship could be erected.

How much the Church owes to Lydia! The congregation at Philippi, of which Lydia was the first charter member, was Paul's favorite and did more than any other to support him financially in his work (Philippians 4:15).

Priscilla, a Great Church Worker

47. In the history of the Early Christian Church, Priscilla shines like a star. She was an intelligent, energetic, and unselfish church worker, prominent in the congregations at Corinth, Ephesus, and Rome. Because they were Jews, she and her husband had been banished from Rome by the Emperor Claudius about the year AD 50. Since Aquila was a tentmaker, Paul turned to him for employment in order to support himself at Corinth. We do not know when Aquila and Priscilla became Christians. But they were staunch friends of Paul and did much to help him spread the Gospel. They accompanied the apostle to Ephesus and remained there for some time, while Paul returned to Syria for a brief visit (Acts 18:18). Paul frequently greeted them in his Epistles (Romans 16:3; 2 Timothy 4:19, where Priscilla is called "Prisca").

48. In Ephesus, Priscilla and Aquila met a young Jewish man, Apollos, from Alexandria, who was a brilliant scholar and sincere in his religion but who knew very little about Jesus. They invited him into their home and instructed him in the Christian religion (Acts 18:24–26). Their home could be called the first Christian seminary. Apollos later became a pastor in Corinth (see 1 Corinthians 3:5–6; 16:12).

49. Priscilla may have been better educated or enjoyed a higher social standing than her husband, hence in Acts 18:18; Romans 16:3; and 2 Timothy 4:19 she is named before Aquila. Aquila's name appears first in Acts 18:2 and 1 Corinthians 16:19. Priscilla was undoubtedly a faithful wife; the fact that Aquila and she are always mentioned together indicates that they lived and worked in complete harmony.

The apostle bestowed high praise upon this godly and devoted couple (Romans 16:3–5). At some time they seem to have risked their lives to protect him. He maintained that not only he but the whole Church was deeply indebted to them for the services they had rendered. There is a tradition claiming that they finally returned to Rome and suffered martyrdom there.

Other Women in Acts and the Epistles

50. The story of Sapphira and Ananias should serve to warn us about deceiving the Lord. Both were chastised with sudden death for their lies. Paul notes that such incidents, which are recorded in both the Old and New Testaments, "were written down for our instruction" (1 Corinthians 10:11). If we make a vow to the Lord, we should keep it.

51. Another noted Mary of the New Testament was the mother of the evangelist John Mark (Acts 12:12). All that is known of her is that she must have been a woman of means, a devout Christian, and that she offered her home to the congregation at Jerusalem as a place where the members could meet and hold divine services. Her maid, Rhoda, was a loyal member of that congregation and was deeply concerned about Peter's fate.

The unmarried daughters of the evangelist Philip possessed the remarkable gift of prophecy (Acts 21:9).

52. Timothy's mother, Eunice, and apparently also his maternal grandmother, Lois, were Jewish believers; his father was a Gentile (Acts 16:1). Paul says it was due to Lois and Eunice that Timothy was well-grounded in the Old Testament Scriptures, which foretold of Christ (see 2 Timothy 1:5; 3:15).

53. The poor girl in Acts 16:16–18 was possessed by a demon, which enabled her to make uncanny (and true) statements about people; her skill at witchcraft (she was a slave) enriched the coffers of her greedy masters. Paul broke Satan's spell over her, and it is likely that she became a believer. As we saw earlier in the study about Lydia, this miracle earned Paul and Silas a short stay in the jail at Philippi.

54. All we know about Paul's sister and the wives of the apostles is briefly indicated in these passages: Acts 23:16; 1 Corinthians 9:5; 7:8. Note, however, that it was important to the Holy Spirit that these women be mentioned in the Scriptures (see 2 Timothy 3:16–17).

55. Phoebe was one of the first deaconesses in the Church (Romans 16:1–2). She was a member of the congregation at Cenchrea, east of Corinth. She was the bearer of the Epistle of Paul to the Romans. Paul speaks of her as a true friend, helper, and the patroness of many.

In sending greetings to the Christians at Rome, Paul commends these women: Prisca (Priscilla; v. 3); Mary (v. 6); Tryphena, Tryphosa, and Persis (v. 12); the mother of Rufus (v. 13), who evidently was the wife of Simon of Cyrene, the man who had carried Christ's cross (see Mark 15:21); and Julia and an unnamed sister of Nereus (v. 15).

56. Love is the key to all relationships. In his great chapter on love, 1 Corinthians 13, Paul shows the Spirit-given attitude that all believing women possess through faith in God's Son. That attitude of love, which we have for others because Christ first loved us (1 John 4:19), expresses itself in loving words and deeds (1 Corinthians 13:4–7). Participants should also know that they are "fellow citizens with the saints and members of the household of God, built on the foundation of the apostles and prophets, Christ Jesus Himself being the cornerstone, in whom the whole structure, being joined together, grows into a holy temple in the Lord" (Ephesians 2:19–21).

Encourage participants to review what they've learned by studying the great women of the Bible and to offer practical ways today's Christian women can put the above passages into practice as they are built up together in God's holy temple, the Church.